RELAXING FLOWERS

— Coloring Book —

I Belong to:

_____

_____

Thank you for your purchase!

Your support means the world to us. As a small family business on Amazon KDP, we are dedicated to creating better and better books.

We want to express our gratitude by offering you a FREE GIFT!

*Visit our website **www.gn-press.com** and discover the entire book collection and the exclusive bonus we have prepared just for you as a token of our appreciation.*

Adults Coloring Books	Christian Books
Kids Coloring Books	Activity Books
Notebooks	Workbooks
Planners	Related Products

Scan Here

*If you've enjoyed our book, we would be thrilled if you could share your experience with others, by referring our book to your friends, and family, and leaving an honest **review on Amazon KDP***

Again, Thank you for your support and being a part of our journey.

Your satisfaction is our utmost priority, so please don't hesitate to contact us with any feedback or suggestions.

If you want to order this book just scan here

Magnolia

" The only thing we have to fear is fear itself. "

FRANKLIN D. ROOSEVELT

Pansy

" *Believe you can and you're halfway there.* "

THEODORE ROOSEVELT

Freesia

" The only source of knowledge is experience. "

ALBERT EINSTEIN

Hibiscus

" The only person you are destined to become is the person you decide to be. "

RALPH WALDO EMERSON

Aster

"I am not a product of my circumstances. I am a product of my decisions."

STEPHEN COVEY

Bulbous Buttercup

"I attribute my success to this: I never gave or took any excuse."

FLORENCE NIGHTINGALE

Sunflower

" The only place where success comes before work is in the dictionary. "

VIDAL SASSOON

Marigold

"I have not failed. I've just found 10,000 ways that won't work."

THOMAS EDISON

Orchid

"Believe in yourself, take on your challenges, dig deep within yourself to conquer fears."

CHANTAL SUTHERLAND

Aamaryllis

" Happiness is not something you postpone for the future; it is something you design for the present."

Jim Rohn

Apple Blossom

" *Believe in the power of your dreams and the universe will conspire to make them happen.* "

PAULO COELHO

Anemone

"If you want to lift yourself up, lift up someone else."

BOOKER T. WASHINGTON

Gladioli

" *Don't judge each day by the harvest you reap but by the seeds that you plant.* "

ROBERT LOUIS STEVENSON

Dahlia

"The greatest glory in living lies not in never falling, but in rising every time we fall."

NELSON MANDELA

Bourvardia

"If you don't like something, change it. If you can't change it, change your attitude."

MAYA ANGELOU

Hyacinth

" *Happiness is not something ready-made. It comes from your own actions.* "

DALAI LAMA XIV

Delphinium

" *Believe in yourself, take on your challenges, dig deep within yourself to conquer fears.* "

CHANTAL SUTHERLAND

Gerbera

" Everything you can imagine is real."

PABLO PICASSO

Violet

" Don't watch the clock; do what it does. Keep going. "

SAM LEVENSON

Peonies

" Chase your dreams but always know the road that will lead you home again."

UNKNOWN

Water Lily

" The difference between ordinary and extraordinary is that little extra. "

JIMMY JOHNSON

Chrisanthemum

"*Opportunities don't happen. You create them.*"

CHRIS GROSSER

Laurel

" Life is 10% what happens to us and 90% how we react to it. "

CHARLES R. SWINDOLL

Morning Glory

" *The only true wisdom is in knowing you know nothing.* "

SOCRATES

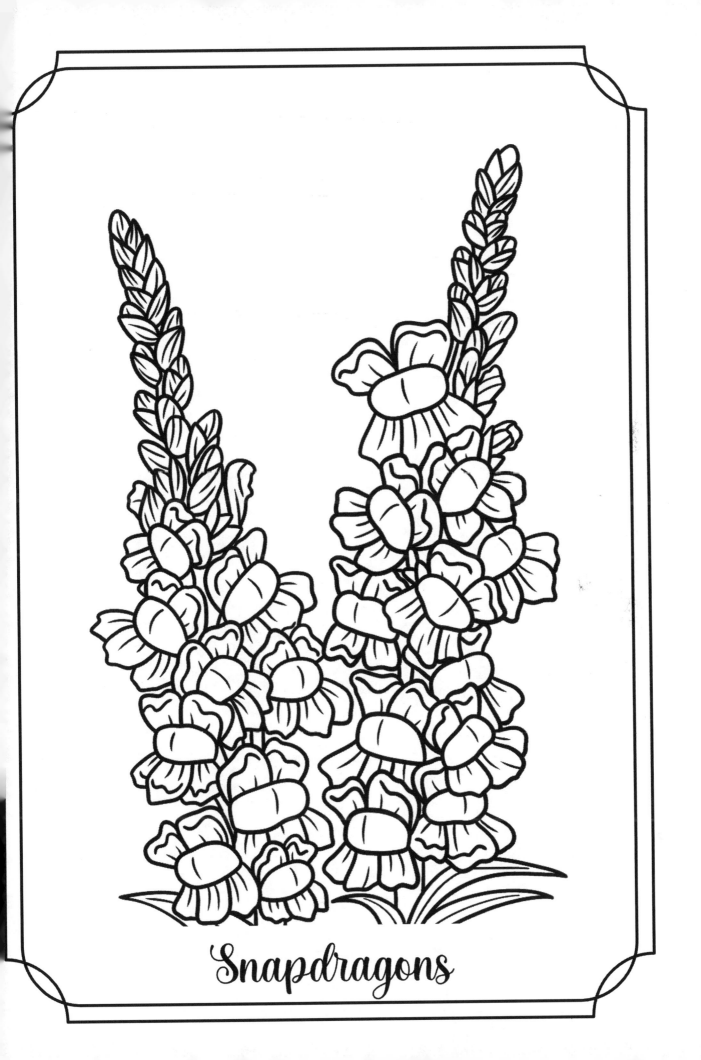

Snapdragons

" You can't build a reputation on what you are going to do. "

HENRY FORD

Begonia

" *The way to get started is to quit talking and begin doing.* "

WALT DISNEY

Lilies

" *You are never too old to set another goal or to dream a new dream.* "

Lisianthus

" Success is stumbling from failure to failure with no loss of enthusiasm."

WINSTON CHURCHILL

Irises

" The only thing standing between you and your goal is the story you keep telling yourself. "

JORDAN BELFORT

Daffodil

" The best way to predict your future is to create it. "

ABRAHAM LINCOLN

Camellia

" Strive not to be a success, but rather to be of value. "

ALBERT EINSTEIN

Jasmine

" Be the change
you wish to see
in the world."

MAHATMA GANDHI

Gardenia

" *Your time is limited, don't waste it living someone else's life.* "

STEVE JOBS

Daisy

" *If you can dream it, you can achieve it.* "

Zig Ziglar

Carnation

" Don't let yesterday take up too much of today. "

WILL ROGERS

Peace Lily

" Happiness is not something ready made. It comes from your own actions. "

DALAI LAMA

Leucanthemum

" When you have a dream, you've got to grab it and never let go. "

CAROL BURNETT

Proteas

" There is nothing impossible to they who will try."

ALEXANDER THE GREAT

Crocus

" The only limit to our realization of tomorrow will be our doubts of today"

FRANKLIN D. ROOSEVELT

Hydrangea

"It's not about perfect. It's about effort. That's how change occurs."

UNKNOWN

Sweat Pea

" *Keep your face always toward the sunshine, and shadows will fall behind you.* "

WALT WHITMAN

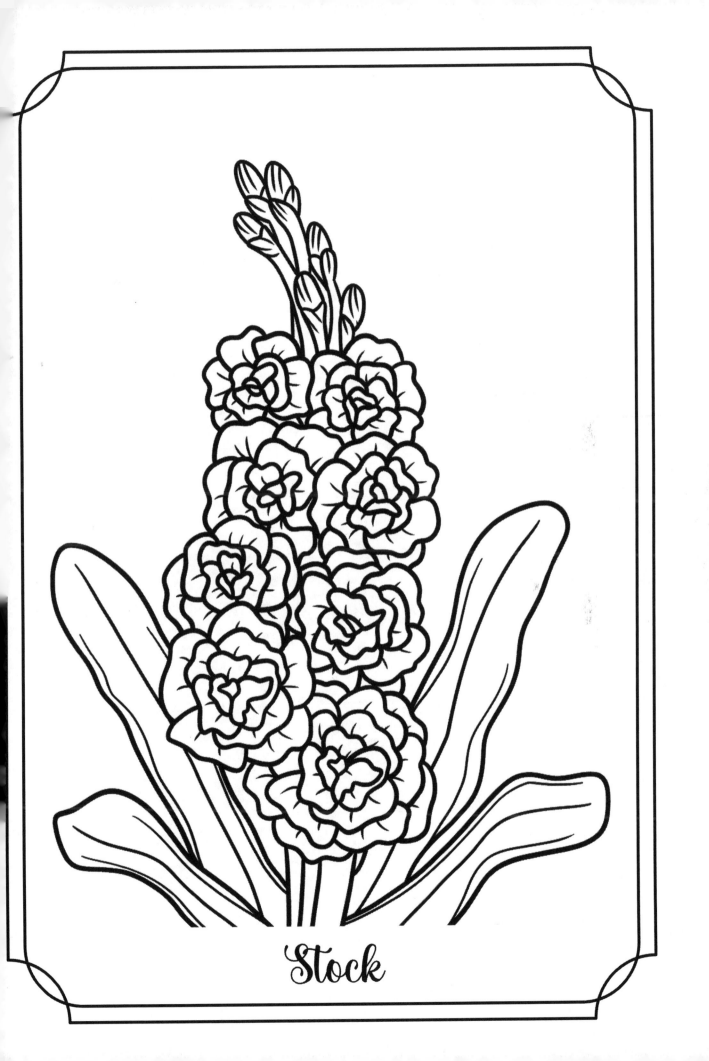

Stock

" *Do what you can, with what you have, where you are.* "

THEODORE ROOSEVELT

Anthurium

" *Success is not the key to happiness. Happiness is the key to success.* "

ALBERT SCHWEITZER

Rose

" *It's not whether you get knocked down, it's whether you get up.* "

VINCE LOMBARDI

Lotus

" The only person you are destined to become is the person you decide to be."

RALPH WALDO EMERSON

Tulips

"The future belongs to those who believe in the beauty of their dreams."

ELEANOR ROOSEVELT

Lavender

"It does not matter how slowly you go as long as you do not stop."

CONFUCIUS

Forget Me Not

" The only way to do something in life is to start doing it. "

UNKNOWN

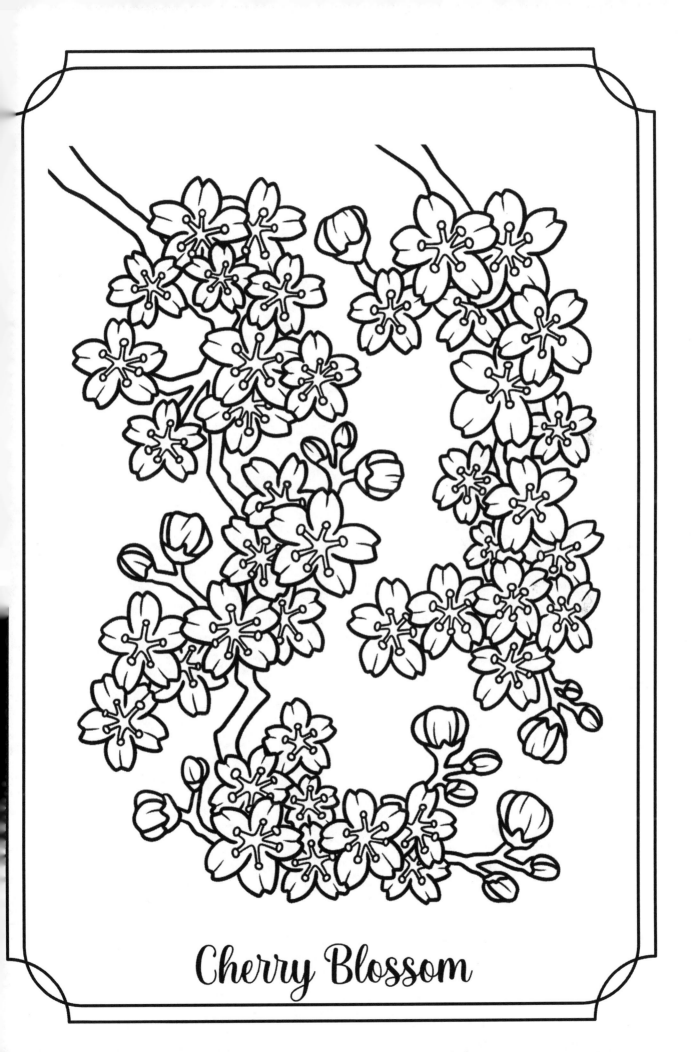

Cherry Blossom

" The only way to do something in life is to start doing it. "

UNKNOWN

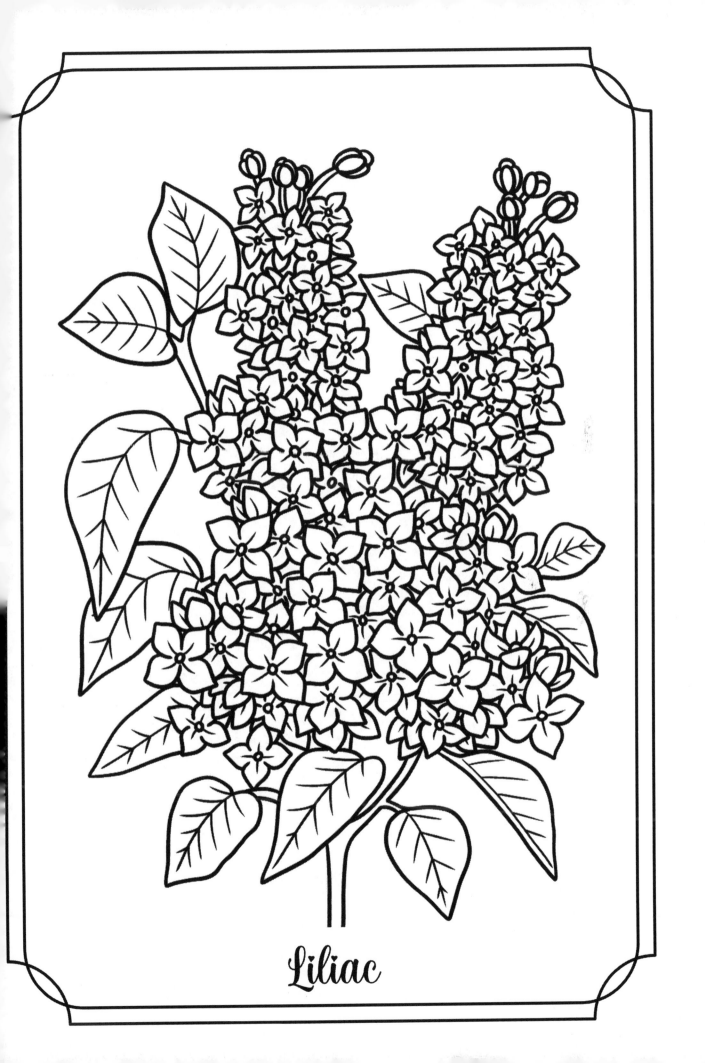

Liliac

" *Believe in your dreams and they may come true; believe in yourself and they will come true.* "

UNKNOWN

Thank you again for your purchase!

We hope you enjoyed our book!

This is a kind reminder for you, to access **www.gn-press.com** and claim your

FREE GIFT!

Scan Here

We are forever grateful to you!

If you want to order this book just scan here

Made in the USA
Las Vegas, NV
10 July 2023

74440347R00057